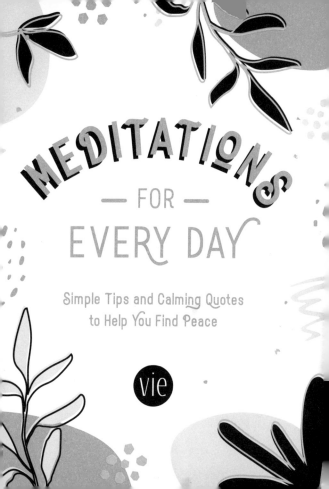

MEDITATIONS

— FOR —

EVERY DAY

Simple Tips and Calming Quotes
to Help You Find Peace

vie

MEDITATIONS FOR EVERY DAY

This edition copyright © Summersdale Publishers Ltd, 2023
First published as *The Little Book of Meditations* in 2016

With research by Gilly Pickup

Purple leaves © Lovecta/Shutterstock.com
Blue leaves © Lepusinensis/Shutterstock.com

An Hachette UK Company
www.hachette.co.uk

Vie Books, an imprint of Summersdale Publishers Ltd
Part of Octopus Publishing Group Limited
Carmelite House
50 Victoria Embankment
LONDON
EC4Y 0DZ
UK

www.summersdale.com

Printed and bound in China

ISBN: 978-1-80007-676-1

Substantial discounts on bulk quantities of Summersdale books are available to corporations, professional associations and other organizations. For details contact general enquiries: telephone: +44 (0) 1243 771107 or email: enquiries@summersdale.com.

INTRODUCTION

When daily pressures threaten to engulf you, look to the inner sanctum of your mind. We all need quiet time to recharge our batteries and meditation is the perfect way to achieve that peace. If you practise on a regular basis, you could discover that it is the most effective, stress-busting technique there is. Better still, it's free, can be done in your own home, needs no specialist equipment and is scientifically approved.

MEDITATION BRINGS WISDOM; LACK OF MEDITATION LEAVES IGNORANCE.

Buddha

A CALM MIND IS NOT DISTURBED BY THE WAVES OF THOUGHTS.

Remez Sasson

WHAT IS MEDITATION?

Meditation is a process of awareness leading to a state of consciousness which brings serenity and clarity. During meditation sessions, the body is in a state of rest and relaxation. When you meditate, you are fully awake and alert, but your mind is not focused on the external world or on events taking place around you. The goal is to achieve inner peace.

LEARN TO BE CALM
AND YOU WILL
ALWAYS BE HAPPY.

Paramahansa Yogananda

MEDITATION IS A TECHNIQUE FOR RESTING THE MIND

The word meditation comes from the Latin words *meditari* – to think, to dwell upon, to exercise the mind – and *mederi* – to heal. The Sanskrit word *medha* means wisdom. When practised, meditation enables you to reach a state of consciousness which is totally different from the normal waking state. The goal is not to get rid of thoughts, but to become more aware of the "silence" that is present in the mind along with the thoughts. It is the means for experiencing the centre of consciousness within ourselves. When we cultivate a peaceful mind, it follows that we feel good and positive within. Meditation brings mental, emotional and spiritual balance, which is the key to enlightenment.

THE GIFT OF LEARNING
TO MEDITATE IS THE
GREATEST GIFT YOU
CAN GIVE YOURSELF
IN THIS LIFETIME.

Sogyal Rinpoche

THE BEST WAY TO MEDITATE IS THROUGH MEDITATION ITSELF.

Ramana Maharshi

MEDITATION BRINGS MANY BENEFITS

Besides reducing stress and decreasing muscle tension, meditation can help us make better decisions, which leads to higher productivity at work. It increases creativity and mental alertness and may aid problem-solving, too, making meditation an excellent means of improving physical and emotional well-being. Some find the best time to

YOU SHOULDN'T CHASE
AFTER THE PAST OR PLACE
EXPECTATIONS ON THE
FUTURE. WHAT IS PAST IS
LEFT BEHIND. THE FUTURE
IS AS OF YET UNREACHED.

Buddhist proverb

ANYONE CAN LEARN TO MEDITATE

The good news is it doesn't matter who you are, how old you are, which gender you are or what your nationality is, because meditation is for everyone. You don't require a guru or need to be religious, and you don't have to spend lots of time in an ashram to learn the meditate is in the evening at the end of their working day, and if practised then, it has the extra bonus of helping to enable a deep, peaceful sleep. Whatever time we choose, the act of meditating provides us with an oasis of calm that is often hard to find in our busy lives. If you or someone you know suffers from a mental illness, meditation should only be used under expert guidance. Should you have any doubts about your personal or mental health, see a medical practitioner.

MEDITATION CAN HELP US
EMBRACE OUR WORRIES,
OUR FEAR, OUR ANGER; AND
THAT IS VERY HEALING.

Thích Nhất Hạnh

art. Granted, some people find it easier than others, and some take longer to get the hang of it because, like any skill, meditation requires practice to achieve satisfying results. However, anyone at all can do it and, with perseverance, will reap the benefits.

YOU CAN SIT IN A VARIETY OF POSITIONS WHEN MEDITATING

Most people think of the lotus position when they think of meditating: sitting cross-legged and placing each leg on top of the thigh opposite. Although famous, the lotus is not necessary in practice. It is difficult for some people to master and indeed, even with practice, some may never manage it. If you don't want to – or can't – meditate while in this position, then simply find a peaceful place to sit in a chair with your back straight and eyes closed. It is important to choose a position that is comfortable for you and that you can maintain throughout your meditation session. If you use a chair, pick one with a flat seat so that you don't find yourself tilting too much towards the back. If your feet don't touch the floor, find something for them to rest on so that your legs don't dangle.

AT THE END OF THE DAY,
I CAN END UP JUST
TOTALLY WACKY, BECAUSE
I'VE MADE MOUNTAINS
OUT OF MOLEHILLS. WITH
MEDITATION, I CAN KEEP
THEM AS MOLEHILLS.

Ringo Starr

WITHIN YOURSELF IS A STILLNESS, A SANCTUARY TO WHICH YOU CAN RETREAT AT ANY TIME AND BE YOURSELF.

Hermann Hesse

FIND AN UNCLUTTERED, TRANQUIL PLACE TO MEDITATE

It should be somewhere you will not be disturbed. Bring your awareness through all parts of your body and allow your muscles to relax, except those supporting your head, neck and back. Revel in and enjoy the calming process of letting go of your body tension. Meditation is the science of letting go and this begins with the body and then extends to your thoughts.

MEDITATION ALLOWS US TO DIRECTLY PARTICIPATE IN OUR LIVES INSTEAD OF LIVING LIFE AS AN AFTERTHOUGHT.

Stephen Levine

MEDITATION IS A POWERFUL HABIT

Besides being powerful, meditation is also an extremely simple practice and, better still, it brings immediate benefits. Some people think of meditation as something you do with a teacher, and of course, some people prefer to attend meditation classes, but it can be as simple as paying attention to your breathing while sitting

in your car, at your desk, on a bus, doing some form of exercise or while out walking. Qigong or t'ai chi are examples of meditating while in motion. We explore these later in the book. You can practise meditation wherever you happen to be. Remember, a little meditation each day helps to keep stress and negativity away.

THE THING ABOUT MEDITATION IS... YOU BECOME MORE AND MORE YOU.

David Lynch

THE SECRET OF CHANGE
IS TO FOCUS ALL OF
YOUR ENERGY, NOT ON
FIGHTING THE OLD, BUT
ON BUILDING THE NEW.

Socrates

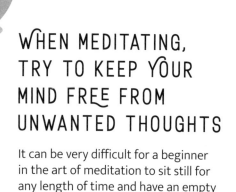

WHEN MEDITATING, TRY TO KEEP YOUR MIND FREE FROM UNWANTED THOUGHTS

It can be very difficult for a beginner in the art of meditation to sit still for any length of time and have an empty mind. Trying to do that often simply encourages more random thoughts to flit through our minds. In general, the easiest way to begin meditating is by focusing on breathing to help concentration and let it develop from there. If your room is artificially lit, perhaps use the dimmer switch to create low lighting, or sit by candlelight. It helps the feeling of relaxation. Tilt your head slightly downward, with eyes open or closed. Tilting your head helps open up the chest and eases your breathing. End your session by sitting quietly for a moment or two and gently stretching your arms and legs before getting up.

MEDITATION STOPS THE SOUND-LOVING MIND.

Sri Chinmoy

HALF AN HOUR'S
MEDITATION EACH DAY IS
ESSENTIAL, EXCEPT WHEN
YOU ARE BUSY. THEN A
FULL HOUR IS NEEDED.

Saint Francis de Sales

BECOME ONE
WITH YOURSELF

With your hands resting in your lap
or on your knees, turn your mind
inward, making a mental note about
which parts of your body feel most
relaxed. Now turn your focus to your

mood, becoming aware of what it is like without judgment. Next, remind yourself that there is nothing for you to "do" while you are here; just sit and let everything unfold. It all becomes simpler the more often you practise.

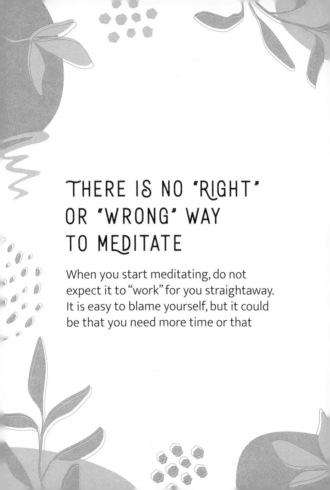

THERE IS NO "RIGHT" OR "WRONG" WAY TO MEDITATE

When you start meditating, do not expect it to "work" for you straightaway. It is easy to blame yourself, but it could be that you need more time or that

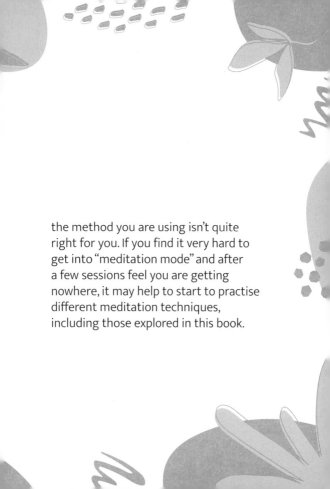

the method you are using isn't quite right for you. If you find it very hard to get into "meditation mode" and after a few sessions feel you are getting nowhere, it may help to start to practise different meditation techniques, including those explored in this book.

LET IT COME, LET IT GO, LET IT FLOW.

Khenpo Tsewang Dongyal Rinpoche

MEDITATION IS LISTENING TO THE DIVINE WITHIN.

Edgar Cayce

THERE ARE MANY DIFFERENT MEDITATION TECHNIQUES TO CHOOSE FROM

Some people may concentrate on breathing, consciously noticing the movement of air in and out of their nostrils. Alternatively, there are grounding and mindfulness practices, which entail simply being aware of sensations, feelings and thoughts, observing them without passing judgment. Others may choose to empty their mind by gently pushing aside any straggling thoughts or by allowing thoughts to float in and out of awareness.

THE PRESENT MOMENT
IS FILLED WITH JOY
AND HAPPINESS. IF
YOU'RE ATTENTIVE,
YOU WILL SEE IT.

Thích Nhất Hạnh

BUDDHIST MEDITATIONS

Buddhist meditation covers various meditation practices which aim to develop mindfulness, concentration, tranquillity and insight. The Mindfulness of Breathing meditation, a basic breath-counting technique, is, as the name suggests, based on being mindful or having an increased awareness of yourself, your actions and experiences. The exercise is simple: as you meditate, count to ten repeatedly, focusing on your breath. Every time you are distracted by a thought, acknowledge it calmly and begin counting again.

Shikantaza, or "just sitting", doesn't require focus on any particular object; instead the practitioner should simply try to stay as much in the moment as possible, observing their thoughts and surroundings.

ACTIVE MEDITATIONS: QIGONG, YÔGA AND T'AI CHI

Qigong, a traditional ancient Chinese practice, combines meditation, relaxation and breathing exercises to restore and maintain balance. It is designed to raise self-awareness and balance life energy by exploring the connection between body, mind and spirit. Yoga is a series of postures and controlled breathing exercises performed to promote a more flexible body and calm mind.

Moving through poses encourages you to focus less on distracting thoughts and more on the moment. T'ai chi, sometimes referred to as "meditation in motion", is a form of gentle Chinese martial arts which combines deep breathing and relaxation with slow and gentle movements. Originally developed in thirteenth-century China as a martial art, it is practised today worldwide. The deliberate, controlled movements and intense concentration required help still the mind and give a deeper sense of relaxation.

A FREE AND SILENT MIND
IS ALWAYS IN MEDITATION.

Remez Sasson

AN AWAKENED PERSON
IS SOMEONE WHO FINDS
FREEDOM IN GOOD
FORTUNE AND BAD.

Bodhidharma

LOTS OF THINGS COUNT AS MEDITATION

Whether you are being aware of your breathing, relaxing by the side of a lake, listening to the birds sing, or simply chilling and doing nothing in particular, it is meditation. If these and similar activities are free from distractions, it is effective meditation. Meditation is essentially focused attention, which when practised daily helps us to draw on its benefits when needed.

EVERY BREATH IS
A RESURRECTION.

Gregory Orr

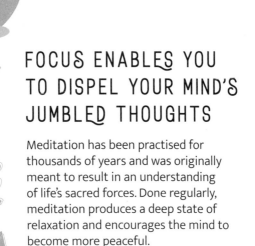

FOCUS ENABLES YOU TO DISPEL YOUR MIND'S JUMBLED THOUGHTS

Meditation has been practised for thousands of years and was originally meant to result in an understanding of life's sacred forces. Done regularly, meditation produces a deep state of relaxation and encourages the mind to become more peaceful.

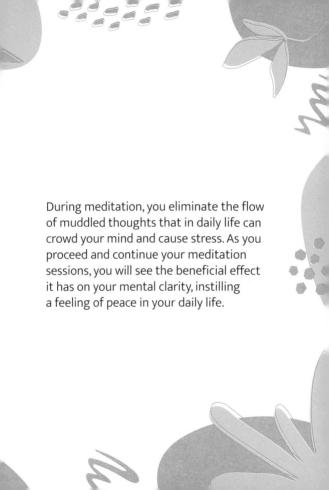

During meditation, you eliminate the flow of muddled thoughts that in daily life can crowd your mind and cause stress. As you proceed and continue your meditation sessions, you will see the beneficial effect it has on your mental clarity, instilling a feeling of peace in your daily life.

KNOWING YOURSELF
IS THE BEGINNING
OF ALL WISDOM.

Aristotle

LIFE IS A MYSTERY –
MYSTERY OF BEAUTY,
BLISS AND DIVINITY.
MEDITATION IS THE ART OF
UNFOLDING THAT MYSTERY.

Amit Ray

TAKE TIME TO MEDITATE

Try to allow a minimum of 15 minutes
for meditation each day. Depending on
day-to-day matters and personal issues,
it can take up to 10 minutes or even
longer for the mind to become calm.
Be prepared to set aside a little extra
time for your session so you don't feel
as though you're watching the clock. In
each practice session, your body benefits
from a state of deep rest and relaxation.

MEDITATE DAILY, AND SOON
YOUR INNER STRENGTH AND
MIND POWER WILL GROW.

Remez Sasson

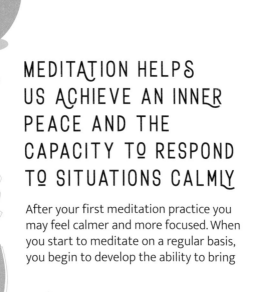

MEDITATION HELPS US ACHIEVE AN INNER PEACE AND THE CAPACITY TO RESPOND TO SITUATIONS CALMLY

After your first meditation practice you may feel calmer and more focused. When you start to meditate on a regular basis, you begin to develop the ability to bring these feelings into practice in everyday life, to study a situation objectively and to consciously choose how you want to respond. The gift of being present and aware is invaluable in dealing with others. Meditation is a fantastic tool for bringing harmony into our relationships, and after regular practice, your ability to harness feelings of calm and to be less reactive to stressful situations will keep on improving.

RELAX WHILE
YOU MEDITATE

Sometimes, particularly with beginners
in the art, trying to meditate can be akin
to trying to fall asleep; the harder we
try the more impossible it seems. One
way around this is to think of meditation
as a welcome opportunity to relax
rather than as a discipline you have to
master. If your attention wanders, try to

practise acceptance and avoid getting annoyed with yourself. Simply direct your attention back to what you are doing and focus on your experience at that moment. It helps to wear comfortable clothes when you are meditating. Avoid wearing anything too tight or material that may be uncomfortable. It is best to wear loose clothing, such as fitness clothing or nightwear.

MEDITATION IS THE GOLDEN KEY TO ALL THE MYSTERIES OF LIFE.

Bhagwan Shree Rajneesh

IF YOU ARE DOING
MINDFULNESS MEDITATION,
YOU ARE DOING IT WITH
YOUR ABILITY TO ATTEND
TO THE MOMENT.

Daniel Goleman

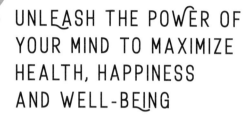

UNLEASH THE POWER OF YOUR MIND TO MAXIMIZE HEALTH, HAPPINESS AND WELL-BEING

People can feel themselves becoming stressed in response to a multitude of daily events, from missing a bus or forgetting a birthday, to feeling they are not up to the task in hand. Although we are consciously aware that these are not life or death situations, the body experiences the amount of stress as "excessive" and so triggers the "fight or flight" mechanism. This diverts bodily resources away from systems such as the digestive or immune systems and towards the muscular and emotional needs. This constant deprivation can have physical side effects, such as a frail immune system. Meditation eases stress and, when practised regularly, will enable you to feel increasingly less anxious during potentially triggering situations, improving your emotional and physical health.

REASONS FOR
MEDITATING

For starters it is a simple, fast way to reduce stress. During most of our waking life, our minds are engaged in a continuous internal dialogue in which the meaning and emotional associations of one thought triggers the next. Meditation helps calm the inner turmoil, getting rid of the chatter in our minds. It can also help improve mental performance, alleviate anxiety, high blood pressure, insomnia and chronic pain, and decrease muscle tension, too.

MEDITATION PRACTICE
ISN'T ABOUT TRYING TO
THROW OURSELVES AWAY
OR BECOME SOMETHING
BETTER. IT'S ABOUT
BEFRIENDING WHO
WE ARE ALREADY.

Pema Chödrön

BE STILL
AND KNOW.

Aristotle

BE AWARE OF HOW YOU BREATHE

If you are new to meditation, you may find your attention drifting away from your breathing. Don't be discouraged. As soon as you realize this is happening, gently focus on bringing it back. It doesn't matter if this happens several times during your practice sessions. As you begin to master the art, you will find it becomes easier to concentrate.

MEDITATION HELPS ME DEAL WITH LIFE'S UPS AND DOWNS.

Eva Mendes

IF YOU WANT TO CONQUER
THE ANXIETY OF LIFE,
LIVE IN THE MOMENT,
LIVE IN THE BREATH.

Amit Ray

MEDITATION IS NOT ABOUT OPTING OUT OF LIFE OR STOPPING OUR THOUGHTS

The aim of meditation is not to achieve a totally blank mind, devoid of all thoughts. It teaches us to clear our minds of unwanted worries and just "be" in the present moment. This means we are not distracted by unwanted thoughts and are able to turn a more intense attention to whatever it is we want to consider – almost the opposite of a blank mind! Similarly, utilizing meditation because you don't want to think anymore, perhaps because your worries are too great, will not be successful. In those instances, perhaps consider other therapies alongside a course of meditation.

CONSIDER WHAT YOU WANT MEDITATION TO DO FOR YOU

People meditate for a multitude of reasons. Some do it to improve their creativity, others to help them to visualize a goal they want to achieve, while some meditate to quieten their inner turmoil. Meditation can often enhance intuition skills, too. That said, perhaps you only want to meditate so that you can enjoy a few minutes of relaxation – that is absolutely fine! Meditation is a flexible art that can help you in the area you most need.

THIS IS LOVE:
THE FLOWERING OF
LOVE IS MEDITATION.

Jiddu Krishnamurti

THE MOST WEIGHTY
TRUTHS MAY STRIKE, BUT
WITHOUT MEDITATION
CANNOT ENTER AND
INFLUENCE THE MIND.

John Thornton

WHEN QUESTIONS ARISE, STAY FOCUSED AND MINDFUL

If you are a beginner in the art of meditating, it is natural to question what you are doing and perhaps why you feel it is not working as you expected. Maybe you simply feel like giving up, or you may even think that you are wasting your time. Be kind to yourself and remember that meditation is a skill to be learned, and, as with all skills, this takes time. Stay focused on your goal and persist. Know that doubts naturally arise in the process of learning, and consider them to be "risings of the mind", to be observed and then discarded.

THROUGH MEDITATION, THE HIGHER SELF IS EXPERIENCED.

The Bhagavad Gita

WE TEND TO THINK OF
MEDITATION IN ONLY ONE
WAY, BUT LIFE ITSELF
IS A MEDITATION.

Raul Julia

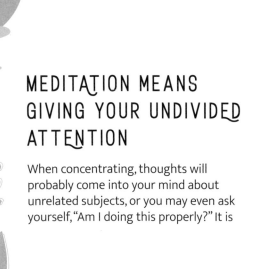

MEDITATION MEANS GIVING YOUR UNDIVIDED ATTENTION

When concentrating, thoughts will probably come into your mind about unrelated subjects, or you may even ask yourself, "Am I doing this properly?" It is

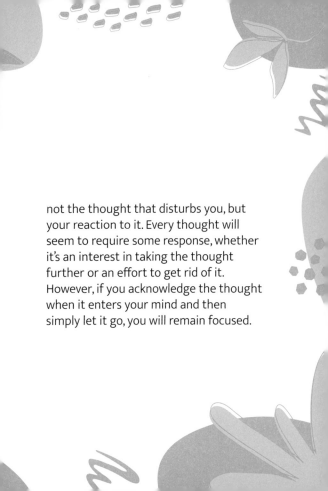

not the thought that disturbs you, but your reaction to it. Every thought will seem to require some response, whether it's an interest in taking the thought further or an effort to get rid of it. However, if you acknowledge the thought when it enters your mind and then simply let it go, you will remain focused.

MEDITATION HAS
TO BECOME YOUR
HEARTBEAT; EVEN WHEN
YOU ARE ASLEEP THE
MEDITATION CONTINUES
LIKE AN UNDERCURRENT.

Bhagwan Shree Rajneesh

LIFE IS REALLY SIMPLE,
BUT WE INSIST ON MAKING
IT COMPLICATED.

Confucius

MEDITATE MORE THAN ONCE A DAY

Try not to regard meditating as something you do as a 15-minutes-a-day chore. Aim to imbue your whole day with the positive qualities that will develop from regular sessions. Some meditation teachers suggest a daily session of around 15 minutes as well as two, three or more shorter meditation sessions of around one or two minutes spread out over your day to revitalize your mind.

MEDITATION IS THE
TONGUE OF THE SOUL
AND THE LANGUAGE
OF OUR SPIRIT.

Jeremy Taylor

MEDITATION HAS POSITIVE EFFECTS ON OUR RELATIONSHIPS

When we feel balanced and calm, it is easier to respond to stresses rationally rather than react hastily or say something we regret. Impulsive or emotion-driven reactions can create harm or upset in our relationships.

Meditation trains you to be fully present with others, helping you listen to what they are saying and have a deeper understanding of what they may actually need or desire. Your responses will be less about the "I" and more focused on the "us" of problem-solving within relationships.

MEDITATION HELPS US GAIN UNDERSTANDING OF OUR THOUGHTS AND PROBLEMS

Meditation allows us to observe ourselves more clearly, which in turn enables us to identify when and why we are thinking and feeling in certain ways. By observing our thoughts and reactions, we begin to notice habits that we may have previously been unaware of. This allows us to make positive changes, and instead of being preoccupied with thoughts which dwell on the past and the future, we begin to live more in the present. After all, it is *now* that life is happening, and this is where we can make changes occur.

PLANT THE SEED OF
MEDITATION AND REAP THE
FRUIT OF PEACE OF MIND.

Remez Sasson

MINDFUL MEDITATION HAS
BEEN DISCOVERED TO
FOSTER THE ABILITY TO
INHIBIT THOSE VERY QUICK
EMOTIONAL IMPULSES.

Daniel Goleman

THINK ABOUT INCLUDING SOME MINI MEDITATIONS IN YOUR DAILY PRACTICE SESSIONS

Besides your daily meditation session of 15 or 20 minutes, try to set aside one or two shorter periods of time in the week for mini meditations. This makes sense because the more you practise meditation, the easier it becomes and the more you will see changes for the better. You may say that you have no spare time to allow more periods of meditation into your life, but if you scrutinize your daily habits you may be surprised. If you have the time to watch any old television show, fiddle with your phone or make a cup of coffee, you have spare moments which can be repurposed for meditation. All you need for your mini meditations are a couple of minutes. Start the process and start to establish the habit. Once you begin to see the benefits, you may want to spend longer doing it. The likelihood if you do this is that you will in fact get more done than you did before you started meditating.

WHENEVER ANYONE HAS OFFENDED ME, I TRY TO RAISE MY SOUL SO HIGH THAT THE OFFENCE CANNOT REACH IT.

René Descartes

THE GATEWAY THROUGH
WHICH WE ENTER THE
PATH TO ENLIGHTENMENT
IS COMPASSION FOR
ALL LIVING BEINGS.

Geshe Kelsang Gyatso

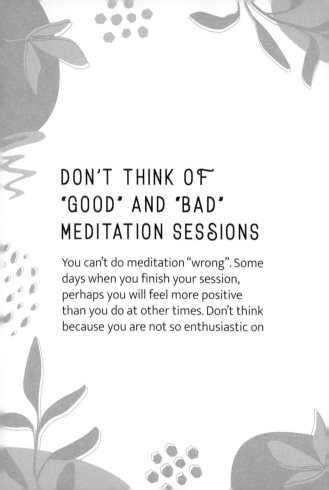

DON'T THINK OF "GOOD" AND "BAD" MEDITATION SESSIONS

You can't do meditation "wrong". Some days when you finish your session, perhaps you will feel more positive than you do at other times. Don't think because you are not so enthusiastic on a particular day that your meditation session "won't work". One individual session isn't as important as the long-term practice, so be assured that beneficial changes will certainly happen over a period of time. One tip is always to remember to be gentle with yourself, never judgmental or harsh.

PUT YOUR HEART, MIND,
INTELLECT AND SOUL
EVEN TO YOUR SMALLEST
ACTS. THIS IS THE
SECRET OF SUCCESS.

Swami Sivananda

THERE IS NOTHING MORE DESTRUCTIVE THAN ANGER.

Geshe Kelsang Gyatso

MEDITATION IS A REALISTIC MEANS OF CALMING YOURSELF

It teaches you how to explore your inner dimensions, to commit to yourself and, with repeated practice, lets you reach the goal of knowing yourself. Knowing yourself leads to learning about why you react to certain situations and helps you learn to react differently in the future. Meditation also helps physically: when the heart, breathing and pulse rates slow down, as they do during meditation sessions, we automatically feel more tranquil.

THE POINT OF
MINDFULNESS IS NOT TO
GET RID OF THOUGHT
BUT TO LEARN TO SEE
THOUGHT SKILFULLY.

Jack Kornfield

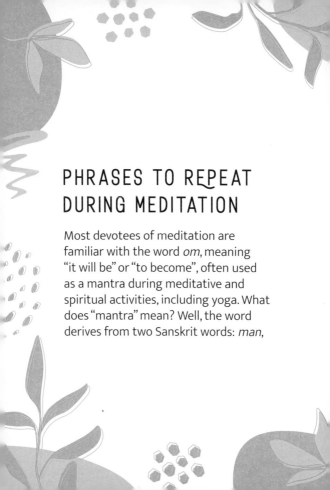

PHRASES TO REPEAT DURING MEDITATION

Most devotees of meditation are familiar with the word *om*, meaning "it will be" or "to become", often used as a mantra during meditative and spiritual activities, including yoga. What does "mantra" mean? Well, the word derives from two Sanskrit words: *man*, meaning "mind", and *tra*, which means "instrument". Most mantras are sacred sounds with specific, positive meanings that you repeat to yourself to uplift you and help you focus. They work on a subconscious level to calm the mind and on a conscious level to nurture the spirit with their positive affirmation.

THERE ARE VARIOUS WAYS TO HELP STILL YOUR MIND

One effective method is to focus your attention on an object, concentrating on the shape and texture in order to block out other distractions. Another is to employ movement techniques, such as yoga, qigong or t'ai chi. These exercises still your mind by co-ordinating your breath and body with gentle movement. Some prefer to use mantra meditation – where a calming word or phrase is repeated over and over, either aloud or silently, and sometimes timed with the breath – to focus the attention and prevent distracting thoughts from disrupting your meditation.

MEDITATION,
THEN, IS BRINGING
THE MIND HOME TO
OUR TRUE SELF.

Sogyal Rinpoche

MEDITATION IS NOT THE MENU; IT'S THE MEAL.

Victor Davich

MANTRAS HELP YOU FOCUS WHILE MEDITATING

Om is not the only mantra that you could use to aid your meditation. There are others, with different meanings, that you may prefer. *Lokah Samastah Sukhino Bhavantu* means, roughly, may all beings be free and happy and may I (the

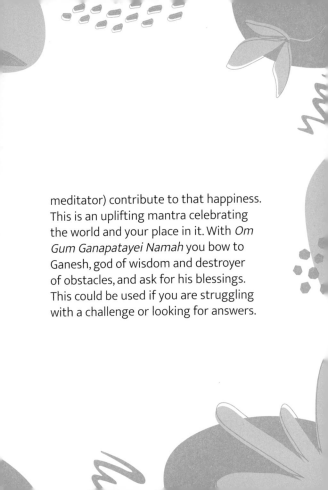

meditator) contribute to that happiness. This is an uplifting mantra celebrating the world and your place in it. With *Om Gum Ganapatayei Namah* you bow to Ganesh, god of wisdom and destroyer of obstacles, and ask for his blessings. This could be used if you are struggling with a challenge or looking for answers.

THE IMPORTANCE OF CULTIVATING SILENCE

We have all experienced the endless chatter that goes on in our minds. Often our thoughts seem urgent; we focus on our troubles, planning appointments or meals, or anticipating a conversation that we may have to have later. We trick ourselves into thinking this is "productive" noise.

While these thoughts can be useful sometimes, the constant "silent noise" in our heads prevents us from embracing peace and mental quiet. Meditation is an excellent way to calm the relentless chatter and enables us to have some mental clarity, peace and quiet, putting aside the rest of our life for a moment and focusing on our own health.

THE QUIETER YOU
BECOME, THE MORE
YOU CAN HEAR.

Baba Ram Dass

WHEN YOU MEDITATE,
THE SILENCE OF THE
SENSES ILLUMINES THE
PRESENCE OF GOD WITHIN.

Gurumayi Chidvilasananda

MEDITATE ONLY WHEN FULLY AWAKE

You need to be wide awake when you attempt to meditate, otherwise it becomes very easy to doze off. If you feel tired, it makes sense to wait until you feel more alert. Even though it sounds counter-intuitive, it is fine, and even encouraged in places, to meditate after a cup of coffee. Or perhaps you need to wait until a particular time in the day, when your energy levels are at their greatest.

MEDITATION IS
THE DISSOLUTION OF
THOUGHTS IN ETERNAL
AWARENESS OR PURE
CONSCIOUSNESS.

Swami Sivananda

TRY MEDITATION AT WORK

Work is one of the biggest sources of stress in our lives, and making important decisions in the workplace is a reality for many of us. Ideally, we are our best, professional selves when doing so, but we are also only human. We may clash

with colleagues or feel the pressure of a particularly impactful dilemma. Using a mini meditation or even a normal-length one at work can really help to calm the mind and focus our faculties. Without the cloud of emotion covering the correct path, we are able to take logical and effective actions.

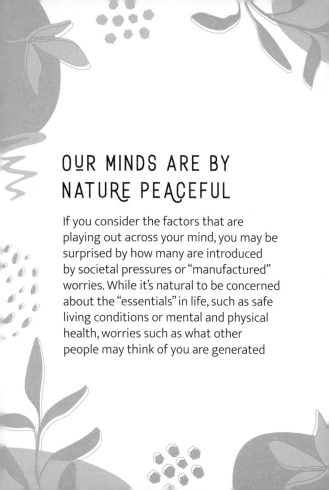

OUR MINDS ARE BY NATURE PEACEFUL

If you consider the factors that are playing out across your mind, you may be surprised by how many are introduced by societal pressures or "manufactured" worries. While it's natural to be concerned about the "essentials" in life, such as safe living conditions or mental and physical health, worries such as what other people may think of you are generated by societal pressures. We often almost look for things to be negative and concerned about when really we would be much healthier and happier if we let a lot of our worries go. Meditation is a helpful tool to relax us, calm us down and make us more appreciative of life's pleasures. It is a shame that we often allow stress and fatigue to obscure the beauty there is all around us; when we are calm and centred, it is much easier to appreciate all that is good in life.

YOU MUST FIND THE PLACE
INSIDE YOURSELF WHERE
NOTHING IS IMPOSSIBLE.

Deepak Chopra

QUIET THE MIND AND THE SOUL WILL SPEAK.

Ma Jaya Sati Bhagavati

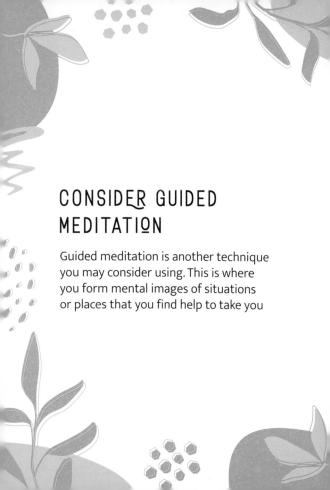

CONSIDER GUIDED MEDITATION

Guided meditation is another technique you may consider using. This is where you form mental images of situations or places that you find help to take you into a state of relaxation. This is achieved by using all your senses – sounds, smells, sights, touch and sometimes even taste. If you do not feel confident doing this alone, you can choose to be led through this process by a qualified teacher.

FEEL LIGHTER
AND HAPPIER

Repeated practice of meditation can not only help with difficult situations and bad moods, but also improve your outlook on life as a whole. It is logical that when your life is less burdened by worry and stress, you then have the mental space to consider what makes it enjoyable.

With your improved ability to handle stressful situations, little frustrations such as late trains are less likely to have a negative impact on your mood, and you are more able to notice the wonder in your environment such as, for example, a beautiful sunset or the feel of fresh air on your face.

REMEMBER THAT
WHEREVER YOUR HEART
IS, THERE YOU WILL
FIND YOUR TREASURE.

Paulo Coelho

MEDITATION IS NOT
A MEANS TO AN END.
IT IS BOTH THE MEANS
AND THE END.

Jiddu Krishnamurti

BE PRESENT

Being truly present in each moment is when we extract the greatest meaning from our lives. Nowadays there is often so much going on around us that it becomes impossible to call a halt to the thoughts, feelings and anxieties churning around our brains. Often we focus on those feelings rather than our experiences and the environment around us. Meditation helps us live in the moment and become fully aware of our choices, actions and experiences. We should not live only a tiny fraction of our inner selves; we should savour the whole of life. Meditation helps us to do just that.

SILENCE IS A TRUE FRIEND WHO NEVER BETRAYS.

Confucius

MEDITATION HELPS DEVELOP YOUR CREATIVE SKILLS

Consider that we all have many thousands of thoughts each day, every day. The trouble is, many of these thoughts are the same ones popping up unbidden on a daily basis. We churn them around our mind, obsessively, again and again. This means there is no space for new thoughts or new and inspirational ideas. Meditation is a powerful practice for going beyond conditioned thought patterns, leading us into a state of expanded awareness and allowing us to open up to new ideas. Meditation creates the mental and emotional conditions in which creativity is most likely to grow.

WORDS ARE BUT THE
SHELL; MEDITATION
IS THE KERNEL.

Bahya ibn Paquda

MINDFULNESS IS THE OPEN-HEARTED ENERGY OF BEING AWARE IN THE PRESENT MOMENT. IT'S THE DAILY CULTIVATION OF TOUCHING LIFE DEEPLY.

Laurie Buchanan

TAKE TIME TO SIT
STILL AND REFLECT

Nowadays we are all so busy that at times
we feel there is simply no opportunity to
sit still and reflect – that it is time wasted.
Successful meditation needs your inner
self to be still so that the mind becomes
silent. When that happens and you have

no distractions, your meditative state deepens and tension dissolves. So the time you spend meditating, far from encroaching on your busy day, can be the most beneficial part of it. Giving your mind time off from the stresses of daily life gets you back in touch with your inner self. What could be better than that?

YOUR GOAL IS
NOT TO BATTLE WITH
THE MIND, BUT TO
WITNESS THE MIND.

Swami Muktananda

SILENCE IS THE SLEEP
THAT NOURISHES WISDOM.

Francis Bacon

KEEP A
MEDITATION DIARY

Some of those who practise meditation
like to record their experiences. It can
help the process, particularly for those
new to the art, because it lets you
see in black and white what you have
experienced and how you felt during and

after. With the benefit of hindsight you can then analyze the session and see what was different that made an impact. It aids in highlighting any distractions that occur during your sessions, so you can ensure you are practising at the best time in the best environment.

MEDITATION IS NOT A PART OF ANY RELIGION

Meditation is to be found in every major spiritual tradition – not just Eastern religions such as Buddhism, but also those emanating from the Middle and Near East, such as Islam and Christianity. However, there is no need for those who meditate to be religious or to follow any particular religion in order to benefit from the practice. It has nothing to do with beliefs or doctrines; it is a straightforward mental technique that can help us reach the inner sanctum of our minds. However, if you so wish, once you have learned basic meditation skills, you can expand your meditation practice to explore more spiritual aspects, such as visualizing a light or an embodiment of your god.

MEDITATION IS
A FLOWER AND
COMPASSION IS
ITS FRAGRANCE.

Bhagwan Shree Rajneesh

THAT WHICH WE
DO NOT BRING TO
CONSCIOUSNESS
APPEARS IN OUR
LIVES AS FATE.

Carl Jung

PRINT OUT YOUR FAVOURITE MEDITATION QUOTES

Choose those nuggets of wisdom which resonate most with you. Pin them on a wall by your desk, on the refrigerator, in the bathroom or somewhere equally prominent so that it is easy for you to look at them several times every day. The more often you read them, the more effective they become until eventually they will seem like second nature.

WHEN MEDITATION IS MASTERED, THE MIND IS UNWAVERING LIKE THE FLAME OF A CANDLE IN A WINDLESS PLACE.

The Bhagavad Gita

TAKE IT EASY
AFTER YOU FINISH A
MEDITATION SESSION

When you finish a meditation session, don't just jump up and start the next activity. Consider what you are going to do next – make a cup of coffee, take the dog for a walk, make your way to the bus stop and catch the bus

to work – whatever it happens to be.
Hold on to that feeling of calm you
created during your meditation; keep
it close and take it with you to your
next task. Remind yourself throughout
the day of the feeling that the focused
attention of the meditation gave you.
Take some deep breaths and recall, and
then notice how that makes you feel.

THE MORE MAN MEDITATES
UPON GOOD THOUGHTS,
THE BETTER WILL BE
HIS WORLD AND THE
WORLD AT LARGE.

Confucius

MEDITATION AND CONCENTRATION ARE THE WAY TO A LIFE OF SERENITY.

Remez Sasson

THE ART OF MEDITATING LEADS TO FULFILMENT

Can you say that you truly feel fulfilled? If you have to stop and think about it, then you probably don't. Are you one of these people who races around frantically, trying to get everything done and dusted in time for a deadline? If you are, then stop! Now that you have read through most of this book, you know you have an ally in the art of meditation. Go to your private space, your "meditation corner", and take 15 or 20 minutes to clear the churning in your head, to focus your busy mind. Let go of daily concerns and allow meditation to bring you the serenity you deserve.

MEDITATE, VISUALIZE
AND CREATE YOUR
OWN REALITY AND THE
UNIVERSE WILL SIMPLY
REFLECT BACK TO YOU.

Amit Ray

MEDITATION HELPS
CONCENTRATION OF THE
MIND. THEN THE MIND IS
FREE FROM THOUGHTS AND
IS IN THE MEDITATED FORM.

Ramana Maharshi

SO, YOU'VE READ THIS BOOK BUT STILL AREN'T SURE IF MEDITATION IS FOR YOU

If you need more convincing, then here are some benefits in a nutshell as to why it makes sense to start meditating on a daily basis. Roll those credits for the following reasons, including: it heightens your intuition, improves your memory, gives you peace of mind, teaches you to forgive, helps you make faster decisions and accomplish more, helps you enjoy better sleep, reduces your blood pressure, gives you increased energy, grants you a richer life experience, improves your listening skills, helps cultivate compassion, enhances your connection with nature, gives you a more peaceful demeanour, enables you to make more conscious choices, lets you discover who you really are, improves brain function, balances mind, body and spirit, and is easier than you think!

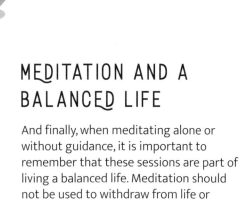

MEDITATION AND A BALANCED LIFE

And finally, when meditating alone or without guidance, it is important to remember that these sessions are part of living a balanced life. Meditation should not be used to withdraw from life or

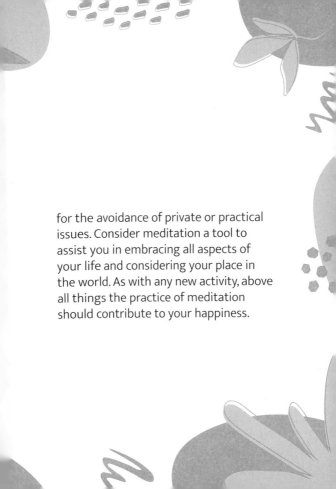

for the avoidance of private or practical issues. Consider meditation a tool to assist you in embracing all aspects of your life and considering your place in the world. As with any new activity, above all things the practice of meditation should contribute to your happiness.

Mindfulness for Every Day

Hardback

ISBN: 978-1-80007-437-8

For many of us, mindful living can seem like something that exists only in other people's lives. But the good news is anyone can practise it. Packed with calming quotes and simple but effective tips, this little book will help you find peace and live life to the full.

Rituals for Every Day

Hardback

ISBN: 978-1-80007-675-4

A daily ritual is an act of self-care that's carried out mindfully and reverently. As well as bringing focus to the present they can imbue your life with a sense of calm and purpose. Within these pages you will find a raft of simple but effective rituals to try as well as short tips and wise words to help guide you on your journey.

Calm for Every Day

Hardback

ISBN: 978-1-80007-182-7

Find calm with this little book. With simple but effective tips to help you manage your emotions and think clearly – including advice on recognizing stress in your body, dealing with anxiety in the moment, mindfulness exercises and self-care ideas – this book will be your guide to staying calm and feeling good.

365 Days of Mindful Meditations

Karen Edwards

Hardback

ISBN: 978-1-80007-101-8

All we have is now. Find time for mindfulness every day with this calming little book. With a raft of inspiring quotations and simple ideas to help you savour each moment and find joy in little things, it will help you to live well all year round.

Have you enjoyed this book?
If so, find us on Facebook at
Summersdale Publishers, on Twitter
at **@Summersdale** and on Instagram
at **@summersdalebooks** and get in
touch. We'd love to hear from you!

www.summersdale.com